REVIEWS

"I think Emmanuel Gaisie's book should be read by all that want to peel the layers off of themselves and get to the root of who they were, how they got there, the damage they caused others, and the work it takes to repair yourself. West and East Coast."

—R. Downing, Correctional Officer

"A revealing look into the human condition. A must-read for all "masters of manipulation" and for those "…who helped make the lie better by reinforcing and cultivating our delusion…" In order to move forward and "…escape the residue of our past." One must come to terms with the truth not as we would like it, nor how we preferred it to be; but how it actually is. Mr. Gaisie does this and encourages others to do so with a cold hard look within.

—T. Hernandez, formerly incarcerated lifer

"Emmanuel Gaisie's book should be required reading for every person appearing before a parole board panel who may be entertaining *second thoughts* at what brought them to prison in the first place. He *illuminates* evidence that denial patterns run deep through us all. The blunt questions are thought-provoking and yield high-value insight, for persons on the journey to recovery and redemption in the era of mass incarceration and thus exodus from confinement."

—Ali Moseley, author of Broken Wing

THE CONCERT OF DENIAL & MANIPULATION

A peaceful acceptance of the truth.

EMMANUEL GAISIE

Copyright © 2020 by Emmanuel Gaisie

All rights reserved. Printed in the United States of America. No part of this book may be used or reproduced in any manner whatsoever without written permission except in the case of brief quotations embodied in critical articles or reviews.

For information contact Authors Inside
P.O. Box 293, Oceano, CA 93475
Email: **info@authorsinside.org**
Website: www.authorsinside.com

Book Cover design by Lindsay Heider Diamond

ISBN: 978-1-954736-02-3

First Edition : October 2020

The Concert of Denial & Manipulation

A peaceful acceptance of the truth

Emmanuel Gaisie

DEDICATION

To all the lives I've ruined,
Especially the *victims of my life crime.

My heart goes out to those affected by the COVID-19 pandemic.

*Out of respect for the victims of my life crime their names have been changed or omitted.

CONTENTS

FOREWORD I

INTRODUCTION 1

CHAPTER ONE 3

CHAPTER TWO 13

CHAPTER THREE 20

CHAPTER FOUR 26

CHAPTER FIVE 35

CHAPTER SIX 40

CHAPTER SEVEN 44

CHAPTER EIGHT 51

ACKNOWLEDGMENTS 63

ABOUT THE AUTHOR 65

FOREWORD

I once told Emmanuel it seemed like he started doing wrong after I came into his life. Up until that point, June 2006, he had no write-ups or disciplinary actions (that I was aware of). I have since learned that my husband was dealing with denial patterns, as it related, not only to his crime but also his upbringing. I questioned him at times regarding his crime when his version of what happened did not add up. But mostly I wanted to believe him and show my support. Thankfully, the story began to change to one that made sense – the truth.

Thirteen years later I can honestly say Emmanuel has begun to personalize the things he has been learning in self-help groups, by not avoiding the truth and facing it. I saw genuine tears for the first time, pain in his eyes as he could no longer deny the truth of his crime.

I am proud of the work he continues to become a better person. I am grateful for his acknowledgment of past actions which have hurt so many people. How his denial and manipulation caused him to jeopardize our marriage. But mostly for being vulnerable enough to share his story with others in the hopes that someone will learn from their past mistakes.

Laura Gaisie,
wife of Emmanuel Gaisie
Author of Twelve Mondays, book series,
Executive Director of Authors Inside, nonprofit.

INTRODUCTION

This book was motivated by the Board of Prison Hearings (BPH) suggestion that I help others using the twelfth step of the 12 Steps program:

Having had a spiritual awakening as the result of these steps, we tried to carry this message to others, and to practice these principles in all our affairs.

Also, the recommendation was made that I should:

"gain some insight into why you was so manipulative not only to the victims of your crimes, but your own wife and family. You manipulated for your own gain without regards to the situation you were placing them in."

I hope my readers will focus on the subject matter and learn from my unhealthy choices and the mistakes that I experienced. I would like for them to reflect on their origin of manipulation and denial. I want to motivate you to seek help before you get a 3-year denial, 5-year denial, 7-year denial, or a 15-year denial.

We must acknowledge we have a problem and accept it is our responsibility to fix ourselves. I wish you all well. We can recover together by helping one another. I understand recovery will be a life-long journey, outside of recovery is relapse and that's not an option for me. Therefore, I am committed to being my best and staying in recovery.

Emmanuel Gaisie

CHAPTER ONE

Initial BPH

My crimes were against *John and *Bill, which were manipulative in nature. I lied to them, took advantage of them, I was ruthless, I was conniving, I was callous, and I was insensitive towards them all. I hurt, murdered, disregarded, disrespected, and did not care about anyone but myself. I was selfish in all my ways. I behaved this way because it worked for me.

The Parole Board's recommendation was for me to *"gain some insight into why you was so manipulative you not only to the victims of your crimes but your own wife and family while incarcerated…manipulated for your own gain without regard to the situation you were placing them in."*

I want to share the commissioner's direct words from my initial Parole Hearing so that you can fully grasp what it's like to sit before the Parole panel and be faced with someone else's professional assessment about your crime, life and time in prison. It's a lengthy excerpt but necessary to explain my reasons for wanting to help you understand the importance of doing your work and preparing for a parole hearing that will be successful.

"The fundamental consideration in making a parole eligibility decision is the potential threat to public safety upon an inmate's release: A denial must be based on evidence of inmate Gaisie's current dangerousness. Having these legal standards in mind, the Panel finds that inmate Gaisie does pose an unreasonable risk to public safety and is not suitable for parole at this time."

"We took into consideration that you are a youthful offender and approvers when a prisoner has committed a controlling offense as defined in subdivision (a) of Penal Code Section 3051, prior to attaining 26 years of age, the Panel will give great weight to the diminished culpability of juveniles as compared to adults, the hallmark features of youth, and any subsequent growth in maturity of the prisoner in reviewing the prisoner's suitability for parole."

When the commissioner gave this opening statement, I didn't realize what he was saying. I was still hopeful.

*"Parts of the brain involved in behavioral control to mature through late adolescence. Adolescent brains are not yet fully mature in regions and systems related to higher-order functions such as impulse control, and planning ahead, and risk avoidance. There's a basic triad there, Mr. Gaisie, the first part of that is diminished culpability, and we do believe that you had diminished culpability as your attorney stated, your thinking wasn't

mature at that age."

For me, this was all legal stuff, but I was focusing on his words, waiting to hear; suitable or not suitable.

"You had been a part of a gang; you were in an abusive environment. You talked about being raised in an area where there was a lot of gang violence and those were your friends, or a gang atmosphere mentality. You weren't jumped into the gang, but you did associate with them. So you had limited control of the types of experiences you had, and it was difficult to extricate yourself.

I think your mother tried to move at one time, but there is a proclivity to finding people that are likeminded and trying to prove yourself as you talked about being accepted."

"We also felt, so we gave great weight to that, that there was diminished culpability. We also gave great weight to the hallmark features of youth. There again, your immature thinking as you made a decision to hang around the people you did. You grew up in that area. You didn't understand responsibility. You were very impulsive, you were vulnerable to negative influences, which I think were probably numerous if you're in a Crip area and you're seeing what's going on."

At this point, I thought things were going fine. I was still hoping and waiting to hear him say, "we find you suitable for parole."

"You were reckless. You had a failure to consider your consequences at that age. We also give great weight to the subsequent growth and maturity, although we do think that there's some work that could be done there. We do see evidence of reflection of positive behavior, numerous evidences of that and the fact that you've matured in your judgment and the way you represented yourself even here today. Um, so we gave great weight to that as well."

Even at this point, I was still waiting to hear the words, suitable.

"In reaching our decision today, the Panel noted that Gaisie does not possess a significant history of violent crime while a juvenile or adult as evidenced by the CI&I or POR, but there is a self-admit that you're in an area where people get in fights and you grew up in a neighborhood where you got in a few...you're no longer 23, you're 48 years old. Also, you've made realistic plans for release and you've developed marketable skills that can be put to use upon release as evidenced by the program that you've done and things that you've taken."

"You've upgraded yourself educationally, vocationally, and you've gotten laudatory Chrono's from those people that are closely associated with you in positions of authority. And you lack serious rule violations in the past three years. However, these are outweighed by other circumstances continuing to show unsuitability and this suggests that if released, Gaisie would pose a reasonable *threat to public safety."*

And there we have it…when he spoke these words that's when it all clicked for me.

"Specifically, we find that you committed the offense to start within a very cruel and inexplicably disturbing, dispassionate manner. Your actions resulted in the death of John Smith and the serious bodily injury, great bodily injury to Bill Davis. You knew these guys. That's what's particularly disturbing, because there was a callousness there, where you weren't stepping into their shoes. You were just thinking about what you wanted."

My thoughts were…It was true, I had a lack of empathy back then.

"It appears that you committed this crime due to the things that you talked about, greed, selfishness. I'm going to talk about the gang, even though you didn't get jumped into the gang, because you don't have to have a name associated with it. When you're associated with a group that is doing illegal things there's a callous disregard for the lives of other people associated with many of those kinds of activities, and I know you've seen your share, and that impacted you…it surfaced in the way you behaved during the life crime."

"So, we felt that anger, that greed, that callous disregard or gang mentality that you had contributed to the reason why you committed those offenses. You possess a previous record of violence in that you were involved with a gang, your family was violent, and you also saw it exhibited by your dad. You had an unstable social history before

incarceration. The Panel recognizes that with passage of time factors such as the commitment offense or prior criminality or unstable social history, any previous sexual crime that you were convicted of or any mental problem may no longer indicate a current risk of danger to society in light of a lengthy period of positive rehabilitation. In this case we considered other circumstances, which contributed to our conclusion that Mr. Gaisie poses a continued unreasonable threat."

I was disappointed because I really felt I had done the work, but I couldn't be upset because I earned this life sentence.

"Now, to start with Gaisie, we do not have a lengthy period of positive rehabilitation. We got an extremely long period of incarceration. We've got a lengthy period of you taking self-help classes, but we're looking for that related behavior that's exhibited in your life, that reflects an internalization of the things that you're learning. So you do have a disciplinary history and that disciplinary history reflects a disregard for the laws within the context of the prison."

"You're doing your own thing. And so that's problematic, because that's a direct nexus to the life crime, contributing to current dangerousness. A part of the disciplinary history you're involved in utilizing a cell phone. And you know, you bring a cell phone in, in the same manner you bring Heroin in, it's the same manner you bring tobacco in. It's a group thing. It's a collaborative effort involving people."

"So, when you contribute to that kind of behavior, you're

contributing to a negative culture that impacts a prison or culture negatively. We also saw you involved in tobacco, and it's the same scenario. You've got to be devious in the way you get it in. And so we saw that same kind of greed being utilized there. There's a direct nexus to the life crime, you're showing as recently as just three years ago. A greed mentality that disregards the rules to facilitate what you want."

"We see that there's a nexus there to the thinking in the life crime. Now, albeit, there may not be violence, although there's lots of violence surrounding those activities within the context of a prison. You haven't been cited for that, but it's the same kind of thinking that we're concerned about is that greed, disregard of the laws that creates current dangerousness."

But remember, I thought 3 years of disciplinary free, and no violence while in prison was good enough.

"You do admit to manipulating people to do that. And that's my concern is because you manipulated the guys you knew back then, you set them up and you had a relationship with them, to a certain degree, albeit, you might've been doing illegal activities, but they'd never harmed you in that way. So, we saw you manipulating him and taking his life, as you said, in a very coldblooded fashion. So, what we're seeing is the manipulation continuing with your own wife, somebody that is very close to you."

"The concern is what's going on there, and that's where we see the work needing. The Panel would recommend you

get no more 115s or 128s, show a stabilized period of time, okay. Take LTOP Denial Management again, and really delve down into it. Denial Management, where you're not being fully truthful with yourself in regard to your motivations and the reasons why you're doing what you're doing."

Questions

1. Can you understand the commissioner's concerns?

2. Are the behaviors you're exhibiting in prison showing a nexus to your crime?

3. What's the general theme involving your 115s (rule violations) in prison saying about you?

4. Mine was total disregard for others, and greed. Have you identified your triggers?

5. Are you willing to make a personal commitment to discover and abandon your defects of character?

CHAPTER TWO

Origin of Manipulation

As I sought to understand the origin of manipulation in my life, I realized as early as eight years old I started to manipulate to get what I wanted. Both of my parents were alcoholics and they gave more attention to their addiction, to arguing and fighting amongst themselves than to me.

I remember at this age, my mother, who had serious sinus problems, sneezed a lot at home. I would go into my bedroom and force myself to sneeze by gently hitting myself on the nose. I wanted to portray that I had the same symptoms as my mother. She would hear me sneezing and say, "that's Nana (the name she calls me) he has sinus problems just like me."

When she acknowledged me sneezing like her it made me feel loved and connected to her. I got what I wanted, which was attention and recognition from my mother. But I manipulated the situation to get my needs met. This is how my manipulative ways began, and it quickly escalated to more serious episodes throughout my life.

I was born in West Africa, Ghana. Living here in America being foreign-born I lost my true identity through assimilation with the black American culture. Growing up in the '70s and early '80s in the inner city of Los Angeles California, I was called a lot of derogatory names; African booty scratcher, Mandingo, Kunta Kentay, Black Buddha. This was because I was from a different country and spoke with an accent. Being verbally and physically bullied by kids at school and in the neighborhood was expulsion because I denied myself.

I told myself I was an American, and not from Africa. I started to believe that lie which made it easier for me to lie to others. I was neglected inside the household by my mom and dad. They would fight like cats and dogs at least 4 to 5 times a week amongst themselves. I wanted my parent's attention, but they gave more attention to their addiction than me. I knew they loved me by them providing for me. They put food on the table, clothes on my back moved me out of Los Angeles to escape the gang influences. I still wanted to feel their love because my parents were not very affectionate.

I do not remember growing up hearing my parents

saying, "I love you," or giving hugs. It seemed like that was hard to say and do for them. As a kid, I felt if I did not go out of my way to make people laugh, they would not like me. I was lost without direction. I was always self-doubting, unsure of myself, and lacked confidence. So, I would go on the defense quickly to prevent myself from getting hurt. I had to fight to survive as a kid in this world to keep from being taken advantage of.

I remember in the third grade at elementary school the teacher asked me to give my perspective on what it is like to be in America, being though I am from Africa. I had no idea what that was, so I just made something up. I do not even remember what I blurted out. All I remember was my classmate's laughter, as well as the teacher, from my response. Since that day I developed an obsession to identify myself as a Black American as opposed to being a foreigner.

Being foreign was very abusive to me. I felt powerless, angry, frustrated, and confused. I believed the only way for me to cope was to gravitate to the negative peer associations. They filled my need to belong and be wanted and loved, things I wasn't getting at home. I had the mentality no one cared about me, so why should I care about anyone else. Nothing else mattered to me but being accepted.

My causative factors then at the time of these crimes were lack of empathy and normalizing violence. I had a criminal and gang mentality. I was irresponsible, immature, reckless, manipulative, angry, resentful, jealous, greedy, shame, and low self-esteem.

Now after reviewing my past, I understand how shame was the root cause of my causative factors. I was ashamed of who I was inside and outside my household. Being verbally and physically bullied by the kids at school and in my neighborhood because I was from Africa, Ghana, and spoke with an accent, caused me to feel shame and hurt of who I am.

Inside the household, I was ashamed for peeing in the bed. I would get beaten by my dad for wetting the bed up to the age of 12 years old. To prevent from being beaten I would sneak and change my bed linen before my dad woke up. I learned being deceitful at home helped me avoid getting beat. I would lie and be sneaky, along with faking my sneezing was the origin of manipulation in my life.

Manipulation allowed me to control how I wanted others to perceive me instead of them viewing me the way I viewed myself, as a loser—not good enough, a foreigner nobody wanted to be around. When I behaved in a manipulative way, in my warped thinking I believed that people viewed me as cool, accepted, successful, important, and admired.

I learned to be underhanded in all my affairs. To do

whatever it took to gain an advantage over you. In reading, in Sheep's Clothing (Simon, 2010), I was able to recognize that I had a fragile ego and I used manipulation as a shield from the threat of anxiety associated with societal "invitations" to feel ashamed and guilty about me being foreign and not being accepted by people around me.

Manipulation worked for me. It got me what I wanted. As I reflect today, I realize I did not care about who I hurt in the process. I became greedy and selfish for attention and recognition. When I manipulated it helped me to stop feeling bad about myself. I became obsessed to make sure that I didn't feel shame, pain, fear, guilt, and anger anymore and manipulation was my go-to. It gave me control over my life.

I believed people saw me as cool, and hip, when I lied, cheated, behaved irresponsible, reckless, impulsive, or when I finished first in a race or competition, or when being a class clown. I had a double consciousness because I felt I was not good enough at home in my African community or outside the household with the kids. I had a war within my mind.

Understanding the early age at which I mastered manipulation, and the devastating impact it had on my life, I was able to see my wrongdoings and the many ways I mistreated people in my relationships; with John and Bill, my wife, family, friends, and strangers.

These crimes should not have happened because everyone involved trusted me. Bill was a husband, a father of two children, a son, a brother. John was a son, a brother, a working man. My wife trusted me to love her and not put her in harm's way. These people, along with society, deserve better than the behaviors I have exhibited towards them.

Questions

1. Have you identified the age you started to manipulate?

2. What was going on in your environment (inside and/or outside your home)?

3. What feelings and sensations were coming up for you?

4. Who have you impacted by your unhealthy behavior?

5. We are not defined by our past; it's how we move forward. Do you agree or disagree?

6. What are the causative factors to your crime.

CHAPTER THREE

State of Denial

The result of my initial parole suitability hearing was a 3-year denial. I felt crushed. It was not the report I wanted to give my wife and family. In hindsight, now I understand not being found suitable for parole allowed me to dig deeper and reinforce my growth.

The first 5 years of my sentence was at a level-4 prison. My whole world had changed. I went from being free in society, trying to improve my status amongst my peers by having the most money and being the biggest drug dealer to being told what to do, when to eat, when to wake up or use the bathroom. Confined, and constricted. I gave my liberty up at the age of 23, and at that time in my life, I did not understand the magnitude of my crime. I was in a state of denial, Delusional.

After 2½ months in a reception center at Wasco State Prison, I was sent to Lancaster State Prison, LACCSP. This is where I began to serve two life sentences for murder and attempted murder. At that time I lied to myself about not committing the crimes. "I didn't do it." I told myself, and others, this lie so much until I started to believe it over the truth.

During my first year in Prison, I would not allow my family to buy me a television, radio, or anything else because I told myself, "Why should I buy a television or radio if I'm not going to be in Prison long." My automatic appeal had been filed even though I was told there was a 2 to 5 ratio for these types of appeals to be granted. Not to mention the fact that one of my victims survived my attack and identified me as the shooter. I still believed I would get out on direct appeal.

A year into my sentence my direct appeal was denied. So, I filed a Writ of Habeas corpus hoping for a release from my sentence, which was also part of my denial. When that Writ was denied I filed another one because at that time I could not understand that I deserved to be in prison for crimes against humanity.

I occupied my days by playing basketball, going to Church services, and filing Writs of Habeas Corpuses. I had no remorse for man, but through my relationship with God, I sought forgiveness. Although at that time I was not breaking rules in Prison with things like tobacco, drugs, or cell phones, I was not being honest about my crimes. What I've learned through self-help groups, specifically, Terrence Gorski's model of denial self-management training, *(Gorski, 2001)* is that there are four levels of denial: lack of information, conscious-defensiveness, unconscious-defensiveness, and delusional (the worst of them all), Gorski (2001) says this is where you "hold on to mistaken beliefs despite having overwhelming evidence that's contrary to that belief."

The environment around me during those first few years in Prison consisted of a gang-mentality, brutality, and stabbings. Among this population were the people I would find to help me write and file my Writs. My first Writ was with a lawyer, and two additional writs were done by "legal beagles," or what was called, "prison attorneys." Inmates who were familiar enough with the law would file writs for other inmates as a hustle. These individuals never asked or questioned what I said, they believed my story. Some even helped to make the lie better. Reinforcing and cultivating my delusion.

I focused on my program while waiting to go home, but there was never a moment that I was not thinking about going home. Each year I had high hopes that my appeal would be granted. Now that I reflect on that period of my life, I recall receiving a letter from my mother (who recently passed on June 28, 2019). She said my family wanted to help me but couldn't help if I wasn't being honest and telling them the truth. She asked me to stop keeping her and my family in the dark about my case. At that time, I would not tell my family anything about my case.

I have a lot of regrets because of my denial. Not only the impact it left on John and Bill's family, but also my family as well. My mother went to her grave knowing that her son was still in prison, which was a direct result of my poor choices and actions. The residue of my past still showing up today.

Then my denial was working for me, and with denial, I learned to manipulate. This is where the concert begins. The only way to continue a faulty set of beliefs was to get people to believe my story. During those years anyone I encountered was unknowingly invited to the performance. My denial and manipulation were in concert together like a musical concert.

Under Code Civ. Proc. § 391(b), a vexatious litigant is a term District Attorney's use for someone who files an excessive amount of writ habeas corpus, (which means harassing and annoying). Quest for freedom was my theme. Every year I kept something in the courts pending, all the way up to the year 2014. I was told that my excessive Writs were a waste of taxpayer's money.

In my warped mentality, the court system were the ones who were harassing and annoying for trying to stop the truth from coming out. And the truth was I was delusional. I was holding on to a mistaken belief despite overwhelming evidence that is contrary to that belief. Me trying to convince others that I didn't do the crime, or it was self-defense, was a denial pattern. I told myself this lie over and over until I believed it.

Looking back now, I was avoiding thinking and talking about the truth about my situation. I was guilty, in prison for a horrific crime. I put a family through hell, and I was trying to avoid the truth because of my shame and guilt. I told myself my crime was self-defense. Then other times I would say I didn't do it. I was not being truthful; I was in a state of denial. I am in prison, serving a life sentence, for something I deserve to be in prison for.

Questions

1. Are you in denial about your crimes?

2. If so, what stage of denial are you in?

3. What are your denial patterns?

4. What did you notice that was unhealthy in my thinking? Do you see some of these patterns in your thinking?

5. Have you been truthfully honest with yourself? If so, this is the first step to recovery.

CHAPTER FOUR

Without Regard

On April 28, 2020, I celebrated my 13th wedding anniversary. Thinking back to the year 2000, five years before Laura became my wife, marriage was something I always wanted. There was never a time I did not think about being in a relationship during my life sentence. Being incarcerated didn't seem like it should be a barrier to have what I wanted. Just any woman wouldn't do for me. I was looking for a genuine relationship, with a woman who loved the Lord first – something I never had. To me, a woman who loved God first would love me second. I would be next in line.

I created an Inmate profile in 2005, hopeful and excited for the chance to start communication with a woman, maybe leading to a relationship. I never expected to connect with someone from my past. The woman who reached out to me was someone I met in Covina, California, years before my crime in 1990.

We knew each other casually - me a college student

playing basketball, she was living on her own, trying to make a living without her family who was in New Jersey. When we parted ways three years later our lives took different paths, neither one of us expected to reconnect years later, especially not with me being in prison.

Laura responded to my inmate profile, shocked to learn where I ended up. It took me a while to remember who she was, but when I realized it was the same woman I had met all those years ago in Covina, I wasted no time in seeking a relationship with her.

It goes back to my childhood; I always had a need and obsession, a desire to be loved. I used relationships to fill the void. At that time I had an obsession to have the feeling of love. A long-distance relationship wasn't enough for me. I needed the interaction and attention of someone close. She moved from Texas in June 2006, with two young children, to be with me. We got married on April 28th, 2007.

I was excited on the day of our wedding. My parents and one of my sisters drove up to attend my prison wedding. After the visit they went home, my wife went home, and I went back to my cell. Just saying I had a wife sounded crazy. The Bible says, he who finds a wife finds a good thing and obtains favor from the lord. So, I knew I was going to be blessed, and I believed marrying Laura was a blessing for me.

However, as I sit here today, I realize the concert of

denial and manipulation were in full effect. I did not consider the situation I was placing her in until I took the denial management course. The commissioner's words kept ringing out to me... "without regards to the situation I was placing my family in." To have my wife move from another state, while I was incarcerated was selfish and self-centered. This is a part of denial. The manipulation was me getting what I wanted, power and control, doing what I had to do to get my needs met.

I had unconscious defensiveness about my behavior because I normalized it for so long, not knowing that my behavior was manipulative. All that mattered to me was having my needs met. But of course, I was not aware of it at the time. My intention to manipulate people led me to prison. I was using manipulation for unhealthy attention without regard to the situation I was placing others in. Thankfully, now I have learned to use that same unhealthy energy for healthy attention.

Manipulation is always present, and it comes in all shapes and sizes. It is important to recognize unhealthy behaviors and take time to think things through. That is the goal of denial management, taking time to think things through.

When I examined my intentions, now the reaction I get is more inviting. In the past when I did not examine my intentions and acted blindly, I invited unhealthy reactions: I got into fights, eventually got a life sentence. I impacted people's lives and caused hell. I traumatized communities and had unhealthy reactions.

Now before I make a decision I think about the consequences and the situation I will be placing others in. if it's going to cause me to have a personal gain and put the other person at a disadvantage that's not having regard to the situation I'm placing others in. When I examine my intentions, before I act, I live a better life. Now I'm getting recognition for being a better person. Getting an education, and I have not had a 115 in over 5 years. I have better communication with my wife, and I am receiving compliments from others. I do my work in silence and let my victory be my noise, and that's refreshing because the results are different now from then. Basically, depending on whether our intentions are unhealthy or healthy will determine the reaction we receive. For every action, there is a reaction, and actions speak louder than words.

After taking the Denial Self-management training I ordered and read a book called, In Sheep's Clothing, Understanding and Dealing with Manipulative People, by George Simmon, Jr. Ph.D. I related that I had an aggressive personality, which I hid through manipulation. I wanted to win in this game called life, and I wanted to win at all costs. In the case of my life crime, the $42,000 John and Bill possessed was the object of me winning in life. I came up with a subtle approach to manipulate John and Bill into thinking they were going to purchase drugs, but in my mind, I was hiding my aggression so I could murder them for their money. My belief system at that time was it was a part of the dope game, ball and have money, go to prison, someone jacks you, or murders you.

I was like a cat that stalks a mouse for lunch. I used aggression to secure things I wanted that would bring me pleasure. I dehumanized John and Bill. I viewed them as a means to an end because they had $42,000.00. I wanted, and felt entitled to what was not mine, and was willing to do whatever it took to win in life, by any means necessary. But I had to be subtle in my approach which was manipulative in nature.

My biggest fear in life at that time, when I made the choice to murder John and seriously injure Bill, was not being successful with a good-paying job or not having my own business. I feared rejection by my peers and family and being looked down upon. On June 16, 1994, my fear intensified into panic and that factored into making the worst choice of my life, which was to murder John and injure Bill because I wanted their money. I wanted to purchase more drugs and triple that amount by going out of state to Wisconsin. I then planned on starting my own laundry business. In my irrational, distorted thinking that is how I was planning to be successful.

In the case of my wife, I used manipulation to have power and control over her. In my selfish and extremely short-term thinking, being the head of the household looked like me exhibiting dominance over my wife for me to be in control. I saw this behavior at home in my parent's marriage. I saw my dad abuse my mother with other women, he lied to her and had a selfish agenda. I remember when my mother received child support papers in the mail, that's when she discovered my dad had another child outside their marriage.

By seeing this example of how a husband acts in marriage at an early age influenced me into disrespecting not only my wife but every girlfriend I have ever been in a relationship with. In the incident with the tobacco, I subtly convinced my wife to bring me tobacco for my selfish gain. I was manipulative, I didn't think about her well-being, because if I had, I wouldn't have caused her to be in a situation where she had to be escorted by the correctional officers and embarrassed. I humiliated her. My wife conceded to my requests because I used subtle tactics by concealing my aggressive intent. Before she realized what was going on it was too late.

In my quest to further understand manipulation as it relates to my life crimes and rules violation report (115's) while incarcerated, I have deeper insight after reading, In Sheep's Clothing. One of the tactics that stand out for me in my life crimes and 115's is, playing the servant role. While I was loudly professing to be helping others, I was really fighting for dominance, only appearing to be working hard on others' behalf. My actions and behavior were shady, for the most part, for my selfish gain over others. In the case of my life crime, I pretended to be doing John and Bill a service by working hard to connect them with the three kilos of cocaine they requested, while concealing my true intention to murder them for their money by any means necessary.

I devalued their lives. I was violent and filled with aggression, anger, and resentment. I had a lack of empathy, along with a criminal and gang mentality. I normalized violence to get power and control, believing it would improve my status amongst my peers. I wanted to be viewed as having money (which to me was a success), and that was more important than their lives, the rules, and the laws. Back then I had my own agenda and now it pains me, knowing I have caused so much destruction in the lives of others, though knowing this about myself hurts, being truthful and honest about my past allows me to heal and grow.

I was playing the servant role in the case of my wife and family members. Breaking the rules in prison by selling tobacco and using cell phones, I convinced my wife to believe I was doing her a service or favor by making things easier for her as it related to money. I said, "why put money on my books when you can save it by bringing me a $3.00 pouch of tobacco? I can trade it for food and cosmetics the things I needed." I had her believe I had her best interest at heart, but the truth of the matter was I did not value or respect my wife back then.

It was all about me controlling how I wanted her to view me. The same with the cellphone, instead of using the institution phone, because the phone bill would put a strain on them to pay. It would cost less with the cell phone, and they would be able to save money, but it was for my self-gratification. I also recognized another tactic I used besides playing the servant role, I also disguised myself under the seduction role flattering my wife, praising her, charming her, so she could lower her guards, and surrender her trust and loyalty to me.

I took advantage of her because I knew she wanted my assurance and approval. I was wrong to treat my wife this way, and I am ashamed of that person I was. I love my wife. God put me in a position to be a husband and my job is to not put my wife and family in unhealthy situations but to respect and value her.

Questions

1. Reflect on how you used manipulation and denial in your relationships?

2. As you read what type of feelings shows up for you?

3. What have you been doing to get your needs met?

4. Has your actions to get your needs met been selfish and self-centered?

5. Do you pursue good, both for yourself, as well as others?

6. What tactics have you used in your relationships?

CHAPTER FIVE

Two or More

Denial and manipulation play off one another and show up as a performance, the one playing off the other. By using this behavior we avoid dealing with the truth about our situation. Children are very smart because from the start they figure out how to manipulate to get their needs met. When a baby cries the parents or caregivers respond. For me, this pattern escalated to more serious episodes in my life, playing itself out like a concert from the age of 8 years old, all the way up to my life crime, and even during my incarceration.

A concert is when there are two or more in agreement; it's also the ingredients for a gang mentality. I had a gang mentality inside my mind because of my denial and manipulation. What was going on within me manifested outwardly. And like a concert, this mentality drew others who were like-minded. I grew up in a gang neighborhood, and we fed off of each other, having the same mindset. Any activity where someone else is involved and you are breaking the laws or the rules is a gang, for example, involving someone in cell phone use, etc... is the concert.

My first write-up was in 2010 for possession of a communication device. I told myself it would make things easier for me and my family. My mom and dad were still involved in their addiction. There were concerns about my mom's health back then because I knew she still drank. I told myself that I was to blame for her addiction, which gave me an excuse to avoid thinking and talking about my problems. I felt I had to be a provider, and I wanted power and control over my situation.

 Back then no one could tell me that I could not have a cell phone because I minimized the situation saying it is not a weapon. Now I understand that cell phones can be used as a weapon and it is the most dangerous weapon an inmate can possess. When you let other people use, borrow, lend, or rent something you are not even supposed to have you are involving them in breaking the rules. What I have come to understand in taking CGA (Criminal Gang Anonymous), is that a gang mentality is when two or more are involved in breaking the law, despite any great affiliation or enterprise is considered a gang.

By minimizing my cell phone use and saying, "having

it would not hurt anyone," I was not being completely honest with myself. I had a criminal addiction that allowed me to break the rules. In my mind, having a cell phone made me feel connected and loved by my family. Now I understand I was operating out of fear that people would think that I was nothing or would reject me and not want to be around me. If I was rejected then I would not be a part of the in-crowd, which again stemmed from my past experiences.

Me breaking the rules and the law was a direct connection to my write-ups in prison and a nexus to my life crime. That old belief system performing again; doing what I needed to do, to get whatever I wanted to get. The old me wanted people to view me in a favorable light.

I have been in denial and manipulating since I was 8 years old, and now it has been over 40 years. Change does not happen overnight, and it does not come easy. We must be vigilant with our process and trust that we can change. First, you must look at yourself, and be honest. Look at every aspect of your life thoroughly. That is how we start the process toward change. In the past, I grouped up with unhealthy people, now today in my change I make a point to group up with like-minded individuals who are on the same road to recovery. This is especially important for recovery.

I was able to gather many tools (coping skills) by attending self-help groups.: CGA (criminal gangs anonymous), Yoke Fellow, Prison of Peace, Denial Management, TUMI, K.I.D.C.A.T. With all this I now have a desire to want to do better and be a better person. My goal is to be a better person, and always being considerate about the situations I'm placing others in.

Tools I've gained:

CGA: Admit and be honest that my life was unmanageable.

YOKEFellow: Be willing to seek help.

Prison of Peace: Reflective listening, and better communication skills.

Denial Management: A peaceful acceptance of the truth and problem-solving strategies. Take time to think things through.

T.U.M.I. (The Urban Ministry Institute): To lead by example, be relatable to your community.

K.I.D.C.A.T: Identify and connect your feelings and sensations to events.

Questions

1. Have you found yourself involving others in breaking the rules or law?

2. Were there instances in your life where you witnessed family members or groups committing a crime?

3. What are some of the coping skills you have acquired to deal with gang mentality?

4. How have you impacted your community?

CHAPTER SIX

Spiritual Awakening

Triggers are a gift; they are not always a bad thing. They help you be aware of the areas you need to work on. Once you recognize your triggers you can get right on top of it and deal with them. It is a signal or warning sign, like an alarm, this thing could jeopardize my growth. I asked God to help me pluck it out, like a weed in my garden.

I was reading in my daily bread when you come across temptations or triggers to humble yourself and ask God for humility and patience. Acknowledge it and ask for help. You do not have to deal with it alone, lean on your support system, use your coping skills, and trust the process.

For a long time, I was disconnected from my feelings. I lacked the knowledge to be connected and normalized a certain way of thinking and feeling. Criminal and gang mentality was all I knew, the unhealthy part. I did not have the emotional intelligence, but now I recognize and understand my emotions and sensations.

My life crime and my write-ups represented the cycle of addiction, obsession, compulsion, and progression. For me I did not give myself options, it was all or nothing when I wanted something. If someone did not agree with me or did not pick me first my attitude would be uncompromising.

It was not until 2016 when I had my paradigm shift. I received a write-up in June, the same month I murdered John. It could have been any other month, but why June? I felt like God was talking to me. If I were truly remorseful my actions would reflect that and obey all the rules. This is how people will know I have changed, by my actions.

In 2016 I attended a Victim Impact seminar with sister Amelia; a one-day event where sister Amelia brings a mother whose son was murdered through gun violence. I had the opportunity to see firsthand the impact years later how it affected her. The mother's name was Sarah and she lost her son from a senseless act of gun violence.

The floodgates opened my emotions, knowing how I affected a family's life, for the rest of their lives; I was responsible for that. It was me taking responsibility, feeling ashamed, guilty, and knowing the hell I put a family through – for the rest of their lives.

I learned from a Kid-CAT group, (kids creating awareness together), that when you are going through a certain emotion there is usually a sensation in your body that connects to the emotion. I may feel nervousness in my stomach, like butterflies, my hands might get hotter, or my temperature may rise. These are examples of how we connect sensations to emotions. We also learn to give space to the child within us, to understand you went through some trauma, and to start the process of healing.

In my relationships being attentive and understanding (giving them space to be heard) shows that I understand their need to be heard and makes them comfortable to speak without any personal gain. Just letting the other person vent and know that I understand their feelings. This is also a skill learned in Prison of Peace, ran by Doug Noll and Laurel Kaufer (co-founders of Prison of Peace, in Calabasas, California).

Questions

1. What are your triggers?

2. When was your paradigm shift?

3. Is your behaviour today showing that you are remorseful?

4. Can you identify your emotions and sensations?

CHAPTER SEVEN

Concert Over

Since my board hearing on August 21, 2019 I have pondered on what the commissioner said, and I have come to realize that I have been using manipulation as a defence mechanism to avoid dealing with unhealthy feelings of shame, pain, fear, guilt, and anger. My thinking was I had to do something to fit in. I did not know how to ask for help. I did not accept myself and I felt inadequate. I am convinced you cannot solve a problem with the same mindset that you started the problem with in the first place. Our recovery must begin with a change in mindset.

My mindset then was I had a big and fragile ego. Egomaniacal thinking is feeling like things are owed to you instead of working and getting a job. I had quick and easy thinking. Most of the time I wanted to hurry up and get things the fastest way possible, regardless of who I hurt in the process. I call this quick-and-easy thinking. My egomaniacal was I thought things were owed to me instead of working for it, I took things. I had a criminal and gang mentality. This was a sense of entitlement.

Me growing up in Los Angeles in a gang environment, I positioned myself with gang members because I wanted their approval and acceptance. I developed the mentality of a gang member, which was reckless, destructive, and not caring about who I hurt, a total lack of empathy.

Taking Criminal Gang Member Anonymous I was able to understand a gang is described as when two or more individuals are involved in a criminal enterprise or breaking the rules, that type of thinking is what concerned the commissioner at my board hearing. That destructive and selfish thinking of a gang member. Me involving other people in breaking the rules and laws. I was shameful of my identity as an African, because of the response I received from the kids, and I feared not being accepted. Manipulation was my defence which led me to gravitate towards gang members and a life of crime.

I had an obsession to prove to these kids that I was no different from them. This contributing factor led me to sell drugs, stealing bicycles, shoplift, lying, and fighting. I wanted these kids to know I was cool too. I wanted a sense of belonging. I became greedy and selfish for attention and recognition. I had total disregard for anyone. I callously and viciously murdered John in a cold-blooded manner, and seriously injured Bill.

This thinking continued while in prison. I received three 115's (rules violation report). The mentality of disregarding others still existed. I involved others in my rule violations, including my own wife and family for my own selfish gain. Me selling tobacco or using cell phones in prison is the same thinking and behaviours that led me to prison. My prison conduct had the potential for violence.

The correlation between my life crime and my 115's in prison stands out to me. I can see and understand when I disregarded the law and decided to murder John in cold blood, and seriously injured Bill is the same thinking and behaviour when I disregarded the rules in prison to sell tobacco and use cell phones. In this prison context breaking the rules is the same as breaking the law, and when I appeared in front of the BPH I had just violated a rule 3 years and two months ago.

My belief system was learned through being in a dysfunctional household and being in a gang environment, which was filled with fighting, arguing, and violence. I had irrational and distorted thinking. It was my way or no way mentality. Step 6 of CGA (Criminal gang member Anonymous) helped me the most.

> Step 6: "we made a personal commitment to let go of our defects of character, to practice decent reasonable conduct through daily actions and behaviour."

What that looks like in my life is when I encounter someone who is walking too slow to my liking when I am trying to get to work or walking to my destination. The person might have a cane to help aid him, or that person might be using crutches. Instead of passing that person up in a hurry, I slow down and allow that person space to walk ahead of me by at least five steps. This helps me to work on being patient. Or when I am speaking too fast and start stuttering, I recognize it and then I tell myself to slow down and breathe to finish my sentence without stuttering. This is how I practice letting go of my defect of character and put it into practice daily.

What stood out for me in the Denial Self-Management training curriculum is manipulation. Manipulation is a denial pattern. Denial is part of the human condition. I do not say this to make light of denial. I say this to say that something can be done about it to fix it. I do not have to feel defeated, ashamed, or powerless of this condition.

In concert with others while I am breaking the laws and rules. This type of thinking is a criminal and gang mentality, but I realized it worked for me. It gave me a sense of control and power that I did not have in my personal life. Manipulation helped me to avoid the pain, shame, and fear of dealing with my problems without regard to who I hurt, or the situation I put them in.

Using Terrence T. Gorski's model of Denial Management counselling, whether I liked it or not I was able to admit that I have a fragile ego that was easily hurt when I made mistakes. I started believing my lies. I told and convinced myself that I was an American, and no one could not tell me that I was not. I told myself this lie repeatedly for damn near all my life. I am 48 going on 49 years old, so about for forty-one years I lied to myself about me being born in America and I believed it to the point of me being delusional. I was holding on to a mistaken belief despite overwhelming evidence contrary to that belief. I wanted attention at all costs, even at age 8, that started at home.

I now understand the damage I caused. By taking the Denial Self Training Management (DSTM) counseling curriculum by Terrance Gorski, and sitting down with a certified Denial Management Specialist, Otis Green, III, for 108 hours, and also reading, In Sheep's Clothing, by George Simon, Jr., if I lie, or disregard others or the rules and laws, I am being manipulative and demonstrating a lack of remorse based on the previous damages I've caused in the lives of others.

Shame, pain, fear, and guilt were the emotional drivers behind my manipulation. The BPH (Board of Prison Hearings) commissioner suggested I take a denial management course to help me gain some insight into manipulation as it relates to my life crimes, my wife, and family while I was incarcerated.

I want to thank the commissioner for his suggestion. It allowed me to see things connected in my life in ways that I did not see before, gaining a deeper understanding of self. I learned about the five components of self: self-identification, presentation, positioning, mentality, and conduct.

My self-identification was, I am an American. My presentation to the world was I am violent, ruthless, callous, angry, criminal, prisoner, dope dealer, liar, murderer, abuser, cheater, manipulator. I positioned myself wherever I went with others who presented themselves like me. My mentality was a criminal and gang mentality, selfish, coldblooded, and greedy. I lacked empathy and disregarded the safety of others. I disregarded the rules, this was how I conducted myself.

Actions speak louder than words, so I had to make a personal commitment to abandon my defects of character.

Questions

1. How did you get to be the person you are today?

2. What coping skills are you using today?

3. Who are you?

4. How do you deal with unhealthy thoughts or unhealthy emotions?

5. Which self-help groups have you taken and which have helped you the most?

CHAPTER EIGHT

Moving Forward in Recovery

It's not about the destination, it's about the journey. Your struggles, good and bad days, what you discover about yourself are all a part of moving forward. Your will to sacrifice all for the ultimate goal, that's freedom. During the process, you will discover things about yourself you did not even know. Your resilience, your determination, your courage, your hope. Knowing if you can set your mind to it you can accomplish anything you want in life.

Cognitive thinking is how I operate today, I am in control of myself. I do not want to blame it all on my childhood which played a role. However, now I understand I have a right to choose what to do when unhealthy thoughts arise, I can quickly discard them and restructure my thinking by asking myself, "what's the best thing that can happen to me?" "What's the worst that can happen by thinking this way? or "What's likely to happen?" Then I make a healthier choice.

Now I am looking for a healthy reaction from society. I choose healthy thoughts that give me healthy emotions and healthy actions, and reactions from others and society: This is how I now manage myself. I can no longer continue to be in denial and avoiding my problems. Moving forward we should avoid all unhealthy ways that could impact people. Not changing means losing everything, or remaining stagnated in our unhealthy thoughts, which only results in continuing to hurt people. Now I draw a line in the sand. I put my recovery first. People, places, and things that get in the way of my recovery I don't cross over that line.

I take full responsibility for the conscious choices I have made. I regret the irreversible destruction I caused John, Bill, and their families. I will forever use the horror and pain I caused them and society as a reminder to never again be that violent, angry, manipulative, destructive individual. That behaviour is unacceptable and inexcusable. I permanently impacted their lives, and I know my actions twenty-five years ago is still very much relevant today and will continue for generations to come.

Moving forward from our unhealthy ways, I would suggest you attend groups. If you have not been going to any groups, then you are not being truthful.

Attending groups help us gain some insight and take responsibility, to be honest and learn about ourselves. Write book reports that relate to your crime.

Going to groups and getting an education will prepare you for moving forward. When the time comes for you to go up for parole there will not be much work to do because you will already have done the work. I never dreamed I would get my associate's degree, and now I have my second one, and I feel like I can achieve any goal I set as long as I set my mind to it.

There are many self-help groups to help you with recovery and moving forward. In addition to AA and NA, there are CGA (Criminal Gangs Anonymous), Yokefellow, Prison of Peace, Denial Management, TUMI (the urban ministry institute), KidCAT (the kid we were before our crime and creating awareness together).

Going up for parole you will need to be honest. The past is not pretty. If the past is ugly, accept it for what it is. Just be straight forward. Do not try to make yourself in a better light as it relates to your past. If you are in prison for a horrific crime and you try to paint yourself as an amazing person before the parole board, or anyone else, you haven't begun to do the work. Reflect on the past, who you were versus who you are today.

Today I have started to unravel all those feelings that were going on inside of me. I was harmed in a lot of ways, and I have harmed a lot of people in return. Hurt people hurt. I live with this guilt, shame, pain, anger, knowing most of the harm I caused is irreversible. Murdering John and attempting to murder Bill in a cold-blooded manner is irreversible. I want you to know you can ask for help, address every unhealthy thought and feeling.

As human beings, we are truth-seeking animals, and the commissioner at the BPH encouraged me to seek the truth about me being manipulative to people especially to the ones I claim I love (my wife, and family). To find the truth I asked myself some difficult questions. Questions like, who am I? Do not be afraid to look deeper into your life. Though it may be challenging because you will have to look at some painful experiences honestly and truthfully, it will also be a blessing in disguise. Hopefully, we will be able to understand why it is that we do the things we do. How we are feeling, and how to correct unhealthy actions. We deserve to live a life that is meaningful in a healthy way.

In the past, I would confuse something that felt good as being good for me, and something that felt bad as being bad for me, which is called emotional reasoning. The truth is sometimes things that feel bad are good for us, and things that feel good may be bad.

We must strive to be humble and teachable. Understand that our goal is no longer to manipulate others to make ourselves feel good. Manipulation is false power and control over people and situations. Without taking groups like Criminal Gang Anonymous, KIDCAT, or Denial Management, I can say with sincerity that I could not stop manipulating in the past. By taking these two workshops, I was able to accept my lifestyle of denial and manipulation. Be honest and truthful with yourself. Displaying a personality to get your needs met hurts others and does not benefit us.

Denial is a normal defence against pain, shame, anger, and guilt. Denial is also a way to avoid responsibility. The four levels of denial are lack of information, conscious defensiveness, unconscious defensiveness, and delusional (the most dangerous of them all). Delusion is when you hold on to a mistaken belief despite overwhelming evidence that is contrary to that belief. I also learned fear ranges from mild anxiety to an intense panic, and anger ranges from mild frustration to an intense rage at that point it becomes violent.

Understanding the principles of our manipulation is huge. I say our manipulation because it was ours, take ownership of it. I have a peaceful acceptance of the truth. Let us discuss the benefits and disadvantages of using denial/manipulation. The benefit for me using denial and manipulation was that it helped me to avoid dealing with the pain caused by thinking and talking about serious problems in my life. The disadvantage of using denial/manipulation was that it prevented me from truthfully and honestly looking at my problems. There are two antidotes for dealing with denial and manipulation: having a peaceful acceptance of the truth and problem-solving strategies.

It is important to have a peaceful acceptance of the truth because if we accept something with unsettling feelings, then when a similar or identical situation arises, we will be more likely to repeat the same behaviour. This can lead up to resentment because we are not at peace with whatever it is we are accepting. On the other hand, if we have a peaceful acceptance of the truth, we can sit still and notice what is going on within. We can hear our inner conflict by being still and paying attention to those unhealthy thinking, feelings, urges, and actions to help us problem solve. This strategy helps us take time to think things through, so we will not act blindly like in the past.

One of my problem-solving strategies that helps me manage my denial patterns today, which happens to be the goal of denial management, are the six T's; Take Time to Think Things Through. This allows me to be still and pay attention to what is happening internally and allows me to make conscious choices.

Another problem-solving strategy is being able to learn the twelve most common denial patterns used in the Terrence Gorski model; minimizing, rationalizing, blaming, avoidance, absolute denial, compliance, manipulation, comparing, democratic disease state, recovery by fear, strategic hopelessness, and flight into health (Gorski).

I will be discussing my three main denial patterns out of the twelve. If you want to learn more about the patterns I mentioned above, I encourage you to take the Denial Self-management training workshop by Terence Gorski, it is very insightful.

In reviewing my life history, I was able to recognize my three most commonly used denial patterns, which are manipulation, rationalizing, and democratic disease state. The curriculum asked me to personalize these three denial patterns by renaming them to something that I can easily remember, and for me to describe the renamed titles.

1. For manipulation, my personalized title is, **Winning over others.**

My description of that is, **I know I'm using this denial pattern when I want to put myself in a more dominant position over others without regard to the situation I'm placing them in. Feeling like I want to get over on someone by being slick,**

conniving, deceitful, ruthless, or irresponsible.

2. For my second denial pattern of rationalizing, my personal title is, **Exception**.

My personal description of exception is, **I know I'm using this denial pattern when I feel the rules, or the law doesn't apply to me. When I think I can outsmart or outslick the rules and law.**

3. For my third denial pattern; democratic disease state, personal title; **It's all about me,**

My personal description of this is: **I know I'm using this denial pattern when I think that no one has the right to tell me anything about me. You cannot tell me anything about me.**

Those were selfish, irrational, and immature thinking as it related to my denial. Being able to personalize these three denial patterns allowed me to quickly identify the thoughts, feelings, and urges of those patterns. Now I can manage my denial by understanding what is going on internally.

In closing, the Concert of Denial and Manipulation played a duet together and carried a destructive composition amongst the two in my life. I listened to the musical concert of denial and manipulation since the age of 8 and well into my adulthood. This melody of Denial and Manipulation was the causative factor in my thoughts and actions in the way of destruction and terror in the lives of others as well as myself.

Now I can recognize manipulation in my life and immediately discard that unhealthy thought and restructure it. My personal title for manipulation is winning over others. What this means to me is when I start to think and feel that I must have power and control over someone and win at all cost regardless of who I hurt in the process, I'm being manipulative. Recognizing this about myself, I can have a peaceful acceptance of the truth and manage my behavior in a healthy way.

I hope the experiences I've shared in this book have been helpful to you. I wish all my readers success in their journey called life. Remember this journey is a marathon, so it's very important to take time to think things through and maximize your decision-making.

Questions

1. Have you noticed a reoccurring denial pattern? If yes, what are they?

2. How can you move forward today?

3. Do you have a peaceful acceptance of the truth?

4. What are some of the benefits of using manipulation/denial?

5. What are some of the disadvantages of using manipulation and denial?

Sources

- *Gorski, Denial Management* Denial Management, Terrance Gorski. Published January 11th, 2001 by Herald Pub House (first published December 2000)

- *Simon, Jr. Ph.D., Simon, In Sheep's Clothing, revised edition Understanding and Dealing with Manipulative People.* Parkhurst Brothers Publishers Inc; First Edition, 2nd Edition, second edition is exclusive to Parkhurst Brothers pub (April 1, 2010)

Resources

- **KidCAT** (Kid represents the youth at the time of their crime, as well as today. CAT is an acronym for Creating Awareness Together, acknowledging it truly does take a village to support young people). The mission is to inspire humanity through education, mentorship, and restorative practices.

- **Yokefellow Prison Ministry** - motivates and encourages prisoners, yoked in personal relationships with community volunteers, to examine their lives; experience the forgiveness, healing, and power of God's love; and return from incarceration with a covenant commitment to, and new disciplines for, personal responsibility and contribution to family and community.

- **Prison of Peace** - Through Prison of Peace, incarcerated individuals are led through intensive workshops as they progress through the various program levels from Peacemaker to Certified Trainer, mastering the art of communication and conflict resolution, enabling them to create safer, more peaceful lives for themselves and others, in prison and beyond.

Acknowledgments

To my beautiful wife, Laura, thank you for your support and understanding at all levels of my life. None of this would be possible without you.

Father J. Farou, thank you for challenging me to revisit that 8-year old boy who felt he had to use manipulation to satisfy his needs.

Correction Officer Downing, thank you for your encouragement to stay on the right path and honest conversations.

About the Author

Emmanuel Gaisie is a Christian man who is married and has three beautiful children. He has an Associates' degree in Social Behavioral Science in liberal arts. He is currently working on a sociology degree in human development through Cuesta College. Emmanuel was found suitable for parole in March 2021. He is looking forward to coming home and being a productive member of society and making living amends through his nonprofit organization, Authors Inside, co-founded with his wife, Laura, and graphic artist, Lindsay Heider Diamond.

Other books by Authors Inside

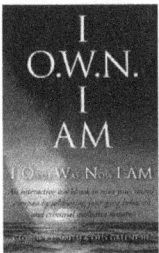

Authors Inside is a 501(c)(3) nonprofit organization committed to publishing all book genres provided it advances our mission statement of, *Making sustainable change through narrative writing, with the purpose of reducing and preventing juvenile crimes, promoting and maintaining safe communities, and improving the welfare of youth and families.*

Submissions should include a one-page summary of your manuscript mailed to PO Box 293, Oceano, CA 93475. An approval committee will review all submissions and respond within 4-6 weeks with a request for the full manuscript if accepted.

Web: http://authorsinside.org

Email: info@authorsinside.org

www.ingramcontent.com/pod-product-compliance
Lightning Source LLC
Chambersburg PA
CBHW060031180426
43196CB00044B/2450